U.S.A. TRAVEL GUIDES

WASHINGTON, DC

BY ANN HEINRICHS • ILLUSTRATED BY MATT KANIA

The
Child's
World®
childsworld.com

Published by The Child's World®
1980 Lookout Drive • Mankato, MN 56003-1705
800-599-READ • www.childsworld.com

Photo Credits
Photographs ©: Shutterstock Images, cover, 1, 11, 27, 28,
37 (top), 37 (bottom); Orhan Cam/Shutterstock, 7; W. L.
Davies/iStockphoto, 8; Red Tack Arts/iStockphoto, 12;
iStockphoto, 15, 16, 19, 31; Ron Cogswell CC2.0, 20;
Everett Historical/Shutterstock Images, 23; AP Images,
24; Giuseppe Crimeni/Shutterstock Images, 32; robyn
CC2.0, 35

ISBN 9781503819917
LCCN 2016961627

Printing
Printed in the United States of America
PA02334

Ann Heinrichs is the author
of more than 100 books
for children and young
adults. She has also enjoyed
successful careers as a
children's book editor and
an advertising copywriter.
Ann grew up in Fort Smith,
Arkansas, and lives in
Chicago, Illinois.

post card

About the Author
Ann Heinrichs

Matt Kania loves maps and, as a
kid, dreamed of making them. In
school he studied geography and
cartography, and today he makes
maps for a living. Matt's favorite
thing about drawing maps is
learning about the places they
represent. Many of the maps
he has created can be found in
books, magazines, videos, Web
sites, and public places.

post card

About the
Map Illustrator
Matt Kania

*On the cover: The Lincoln Memorial and Washington
Monument are two landmarks in Washington, DC.*

OUR WASHINGTON, DC TRIP

WASHINGTON, DC

Ready for a tour of our nation's capital? That's Washington, DC! It's full of places to explore.

You'll visit the president's house. You'll learn where the lawmakers meet. You'll see fireworks and cherry blossoms. You'll ride boats and wander through woods. You'll gaze up at dinosaurs and spaceships. And you'll watch millions of dollars being printed!

Don't wait. Just follow that loopy dotted line. Or skip around to make your own tour. Now, buckle up and hang on tight. We're off to see the capital!

WELCOME TO WASHINGTON, DC

Washington, DC, has streets named after all the states!

Why battle the crowds on foot? You can see a lot from a boat! There's the Capitol, the Lincoln Memorial, the Jefferson Memorial, the Washington Monument . . .

Tenleytown

Highest Temperature: July 20, 1930 106°F (73°C)

Lowest Temperature: February 11, 1988 -15°F (-26°C)

MARYLAND

NW

NE

Logan Circle

Dupont Circle

Washington Circle

Franklin Square

Lafayette Square

VIRGINIA

Lincoln Memorial

Washington Monument

Capitol

Jefferson Memorial

SE

Potomac River

Anacostia River

SW

Some of the city's circles and squares are Dupont Circle, Logan Circle, Washington Circle, Franklin Square, and Lafayette Square.

HIGHEST AND LOWEST POINTS
HIGHEST: Tenleytown at the Fort Reno Reservoir at 410 feet (125 m)
LOWEST: Potomac River at 1 foot (0.3 m)

The Anacostia River branches off from the Potomac River. It flows through eastern Washington, DC.

The U.S. Capitol is the center point of Washington, DC's four quadrants.

BOATING ALONG THE POTOMAC

Would you like to see Washington, DC's sights? Just ride a boat on the Potomac River!

The Potomac River flows alongside Washington, DC. It forms the city's southwest border. Across the river is the state of Virginia. Maryland surrounds the city's other sides.

Washington is divided into four **quadrants**. They're called northwest, northeast, southeast, and southwest. For short, they're called NW, NE, SE, and SW. Every address carries one of these abbreviations. There are north-south, east-west, and **diagonal** streets. Many streets meet in squares or circles.

Take a river cruise along the Potomac. The river is 383 miles (616 km) long!

EXPLORING ROCK CREEK PARK

Wander through Rock Creek Park. Thick woods are all around you. A stone bridge crosses the creek. You may see foxes, rabbits, squirrels, and deer. It's hard to believe you're inside a city!

Washington, DC, has dozens of parks. Some have statues, benches, and flowerbeds. Others are almost like big forests.

Rock Creek Park is the city's biggest park. It's in the northwest part of town. Bike paths and nature trails wind through the park. You can play soccer or tennis there. And you can have picnics, too!

Rock Creek Park covers over 1,700 acres (688 ha).

OFFICIAL BIRD:
WOOD THRUSH

OFFICIAL FLOWER:
AMERICAN BEAUTY ROSE

OFFICIAL BIRD:
SCARLET OAK

MARYLAND

Rock Creek Park

National Zoo

VIRGINIA

Let's stop by the nature center! We can watch bees in a beehive there.

Rock Creek Park has horse-riding stables, tennis courts, and picnic areas.

The National Zoo is in Rock Creek Park. The zoo is home to more than 1,500 animals.

The National Park Service has more than 25 sites in Washington, DC.

You can learn all about Rock Creek Park's wildlife at the park's nature center.

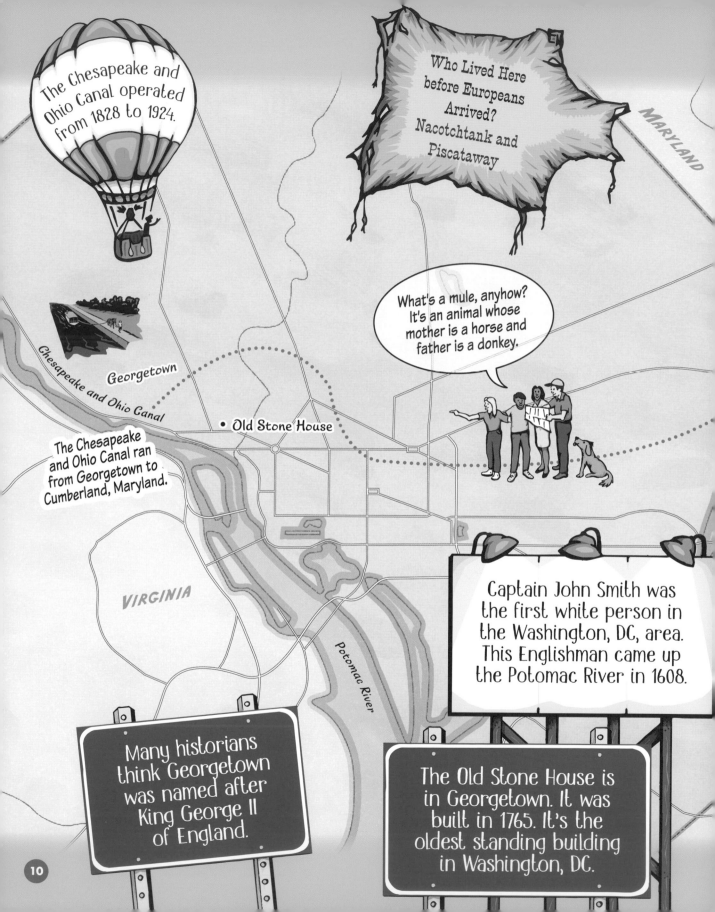

The Chesapeake and Ohio Canal operated from 1828 to 1924.

Who Lived Here before Europeans Arrived? Nacotchtank and Piscataway

MARYLAND

What's a mule, anyhow? It's an animal whose mother is a horse and father is a donkey.

Georgetown

Chesapeake and Ohio Canal

• Old Stone House

The Chesapeake and Ohio Canal ran from Georgetown to Cumberland, Maryland.

VIRGINIA

Potomac River

Captain John Smith was the first white person in the Washington, DC, area. This Englishman came up the Potomac River in 1608.

Many historians think Georgetown was named after King George II of England.

The Old Stone House is in Georgetown. It was built in 1765. It's the oldest standing building in Washington, DC.

RIDING THE CHESAPEAKE AND OHIO CANAL

Head on over to the Georgetown neighborhood. Then hop aboard the canal boat. You'll ride past old storage buildings. And a mule pulls your boat along!

You're riding on the Chesapeake and Ohio Canal. It runs beside the Potomac River. Early Native Americans fished there. English settlers arrived in the 1600s. They began growing tobacco.

Georgetown was founded in 1751. It became an important tobacco trading center. Planters stored and sold tobacco there. Tons of tobacco were shipped from Georgetown's port. The canal was built in the 1800s. It mostly carried coal to **inland** towns.

The Chesapeake and Ohio Canal is also called the C&O Canal.

FIREWORKS OVER THE WASHINGTON MONUMENT

The fireworks explode in brilliant colors. They light up the tall, white tower. It's the Fourth of July on the National Mall!

The National Mall is a long, tree-lined park. It's the center of activity in Washington, DC. That white tower is the Washington Monument. It honors George Washington, our first president.

Washington decided to build the capital city here. He chose the spot in 1791.

Washington asked Pierre-Charles L'Enfant to design the city. L'Enfant's plan called for wide streets. He also included land for parks and monuments.

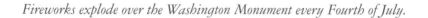

Fireworks explode over the Washington Monument every Fourth of July.

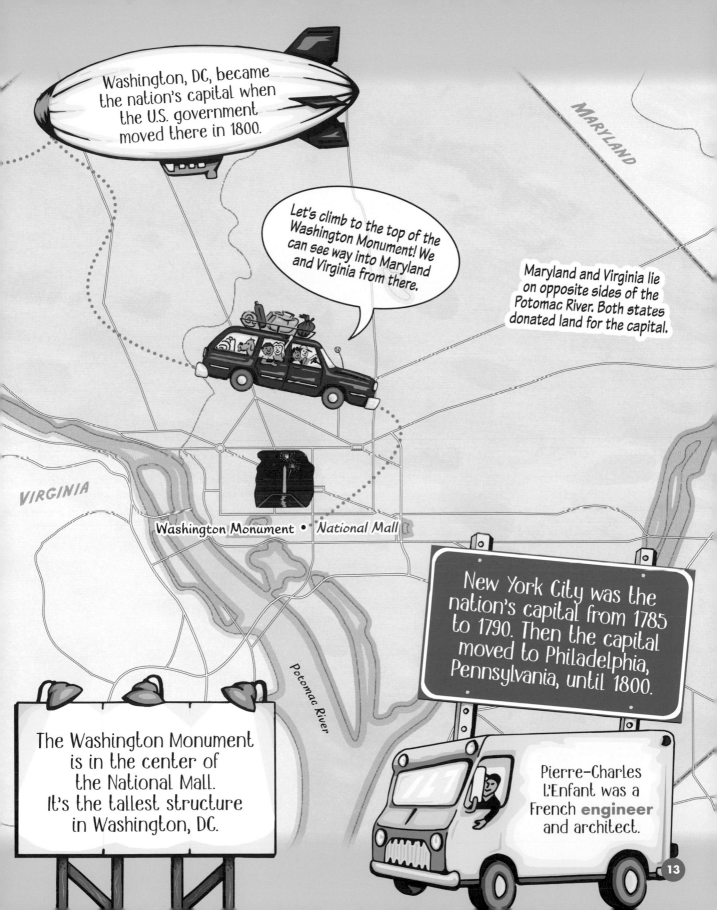

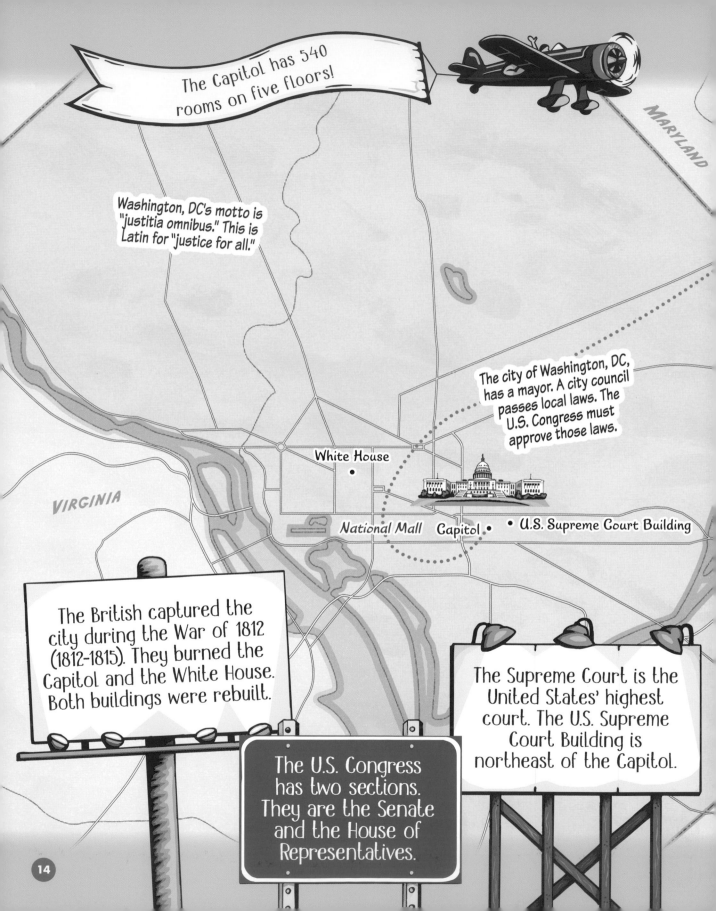

The Capitol has 540 rooms on five floors!

MARYLAND

Washington, DC's motto is "justitia omnibus." This is Latin for "justice for all."

The city of Washington, DC, has a mayor. A city council passes local laws. The U.S. Congress must approve those laws.

White House

VIRGINIA

National Mall

Capitol

U.S. Supreme Court Building

The British captured the city during the War of 1812 (1812–1815). They burned the Capitol and the White House. Both buildings were rebuilt.

The U.S. Congress has two sections. They are the Senate and the House of Representatives.

The Supreme Court is the United States' highest court. The U.S. Supreme Court Building is northeast of the Capitol.

Let's see Statuary Hall! It's in the Capitol. It has statues of two famous people from each state. I wonder who's there from my state.

THE CAPITOL

Face east as you walk along the National Mall. You see a big white building. It stands high on Capitol Hill. It's the U.S. Capitol!

This building is where the U.S. Congress meets. Members of Congress are the nation's lawmakers. They come from every part of the country.

The national government is split into three branches. The lawmakers make up one branch. Another branch carries out the laws. The U.S. president heads this branch. The third branch is made up of judges. They decide whether someone has broken a law.

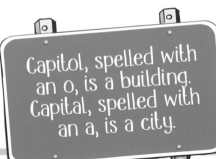

Capitol, spelled with an o, is a building. Capital, spelled with an a, is a city.

The U.S. Capitol lights up at night.

THE WHITE HOUSE

It's white. And it's a house. What can it be? It's the White House, of course! That's where the president's offices are. The president lives there, too. It's just north of the National Mall.

Several hundred people work at the White House. Some help the president with national business. Others take care of household jobs. Guards, maids, and chefs all work there.

Government workers are everywhere in Washington, DC. Government is the city's biggest **industry**. Tourism is an important industry, too. Millions of people visit the capital every year.

The White House didn't always have that name. It was previously called the Executive Mansion.

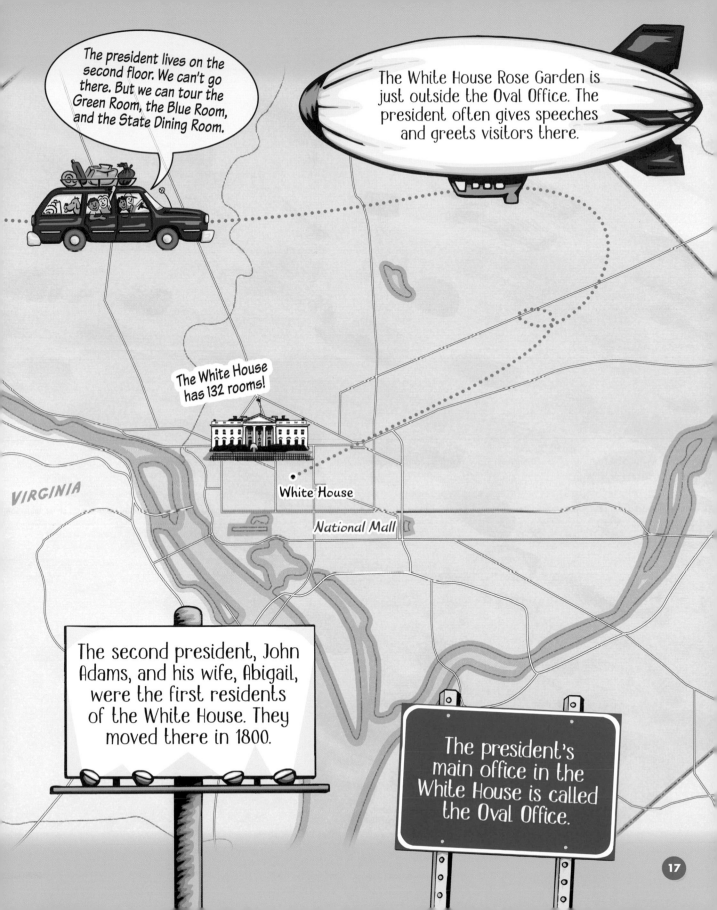

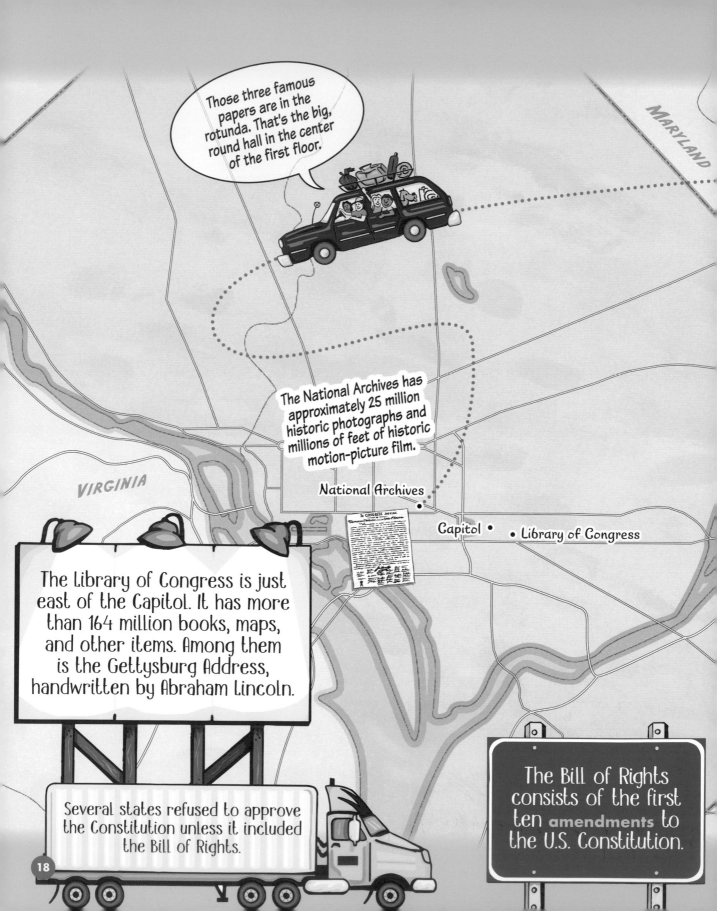

Those three famous papers are in the rotunda. That's the big, round hall in the center of the first floor.

MARYLAND

The National Archives has approximately 25 million historic photographs and millions of feet of historic motion-picture film.

VIRGINIA

National Archives

Capitol

Library of Congress

The Library of Congress is just east of the Capitol. It has more than 164 million books, maps, and other items. Among them is the Gettysburg Address, handwritten by Abraham Lincoln.

Several states refused to approve the Constitution unless it included the Bill of Rights.

The Bill of Rights consists of the first ten amendments to the U.S. Constitution.

THE NATIONAL ARCHIVES

Billions of documents are in the National Archives. This building holds the nation's official papers. But most visitors look for three special documents.

One is the Declaration of Independence. It was signed on July 4, 1776. **Colonists** were declaring freedom from Great Britain.

Another treasure is the U.S. Constitution. It outlines the nation's basic laws. The third document is the Bill of Rights. It promises basic rights and freedoms to all. That includes freedom of speech.

All three documents are very old originals. They're safely displayed in glass cases. They show what the United States is all about!

The National Archives was created by president Franklin D. Roosevelt in 1934.

THE LINCOLN MEMORIAL AND THE CIVIL WAR

The giant statue sits in a giant chair. He seems to gaze out over the National Mall. It's Abraham Lincoln, the sixteenth president. He has his own monument—the Lincoln Memorial!

Lincoln was president during the Civil War (1861–1865). Northern and Southern states fought this war over slavery. The Northern, or Union, side opposed slavery. Southern, or Confederate, states wanted to keep slavery. Lincoln worked hard to keep the nation together. In the end, the Union won. Later all the slaves were freed.

Sadly, Lincoln had many enemies. He was shot and killed in 1865. But he's still a symbol of freedom for all.

The Lincoln statue towers at 19 feet (5.8 meters).

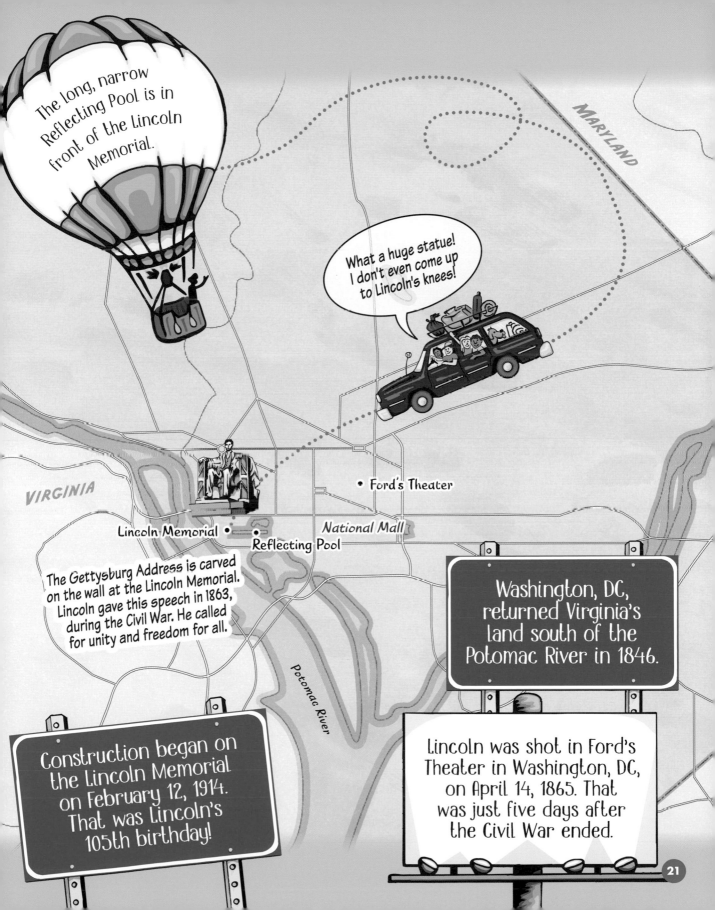

The long, narrow Reflecting Pool is in front of the Lincoln Memorial.

What a huge statue! I don't even come up to Lincoln's knees!

MARYLAND

VIRGINIA

• Ford's Theater

Lincoln Memorial •   • Reflecting Pool

National Mall

The Gettysburg Address is carved on the wall at the Lincoln Memorial. Lincoln gave this speech in 1863, during the Civil War. He called for unity and freedom for all.

Washington, DC, returned Virginia's land south of the Potomac River in 1846.

Potomac River

Construction began on the Lincoln Memorial on February 12, 1914. That was Lincoln's 105th birthday!

Lincoln was shot in Ford's Theater in Washington, DC, on April 14, 1865. That was just five days after the Civil War ended.

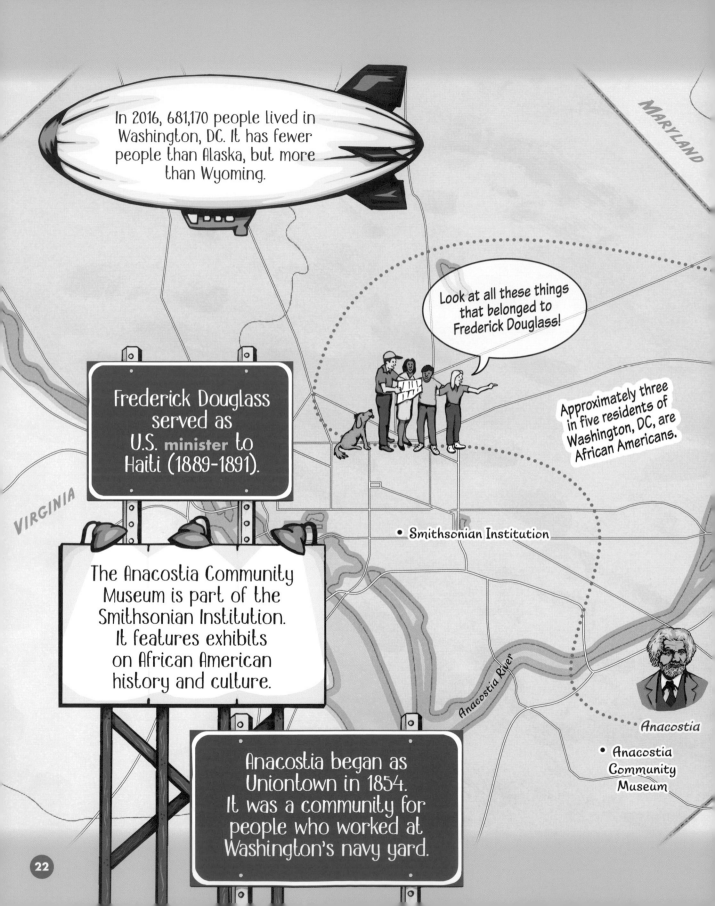

In 2016, 681,170 people lived in Washington, DC. It has fewer people than Alaska, but more than Wyoming.

Look at all these things that belonged to Frederick Douglass!

MARYLAND

Frederick Douglass served as U.S. minister to Haiti (1889-1891).

Approximately three in five residents of Washington, DC, are African Americans.

VIRGINIA

The Anacostia Community Museum is part of the Smithsonian Institution. It features exhibits on African American history and culture.

• Smithsonian Institution

Anacostia River

Anacostia

• Anacostia Community Museum

Anacostia began as Uniontown in 1854. It was a community for people who worked at Washington's navy yard.

FREDERICK DOUGLASS'S HOME IN ANACOSTIA

Frederick Douglass was a slave, but he escaped in 1838. Then he worked hard to end slavery. He wrote articles and gave speeches for years. Now you can visit Frederick Douglass's home. It's in the Anacostia neighborhood. Douglass lived there from 1877 to 1895.

Anacostia is one of the capital's many neighborhoods. Most of its residents are African American.

People started moving out of Washington, DC, during the 1940s. The government began opening offices in the **suburbs**. Today, thousands of government workers live outside Washington, DC. They have homes nearby in Maryland or Virginia.

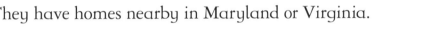

Frederick Douglass is a national icon. Learn more about his life at his home.

GATHERINGS AT THE LINCOLN MEMORIAL

Stand on the steps of the Lincoln Memorial. Look out and imagine huge crowds. Many crowds have gathered here over the years. They come to show unity in their beliefs.

Dr. Martin Luther King Jr. stood here in 1963. He worked for equal rights for African Americans. Approximately 250,000 people came to hear him speak.

"I have a dream," said King. He dreamed that everyone could live as equals. He dreamed that they could live in friendship. He imagined all people joining hands and singing, "We are free at last!" King's words were deeply moving. People still remember them today.

King made his famous speech in 1963. He was assassinated in 1968.

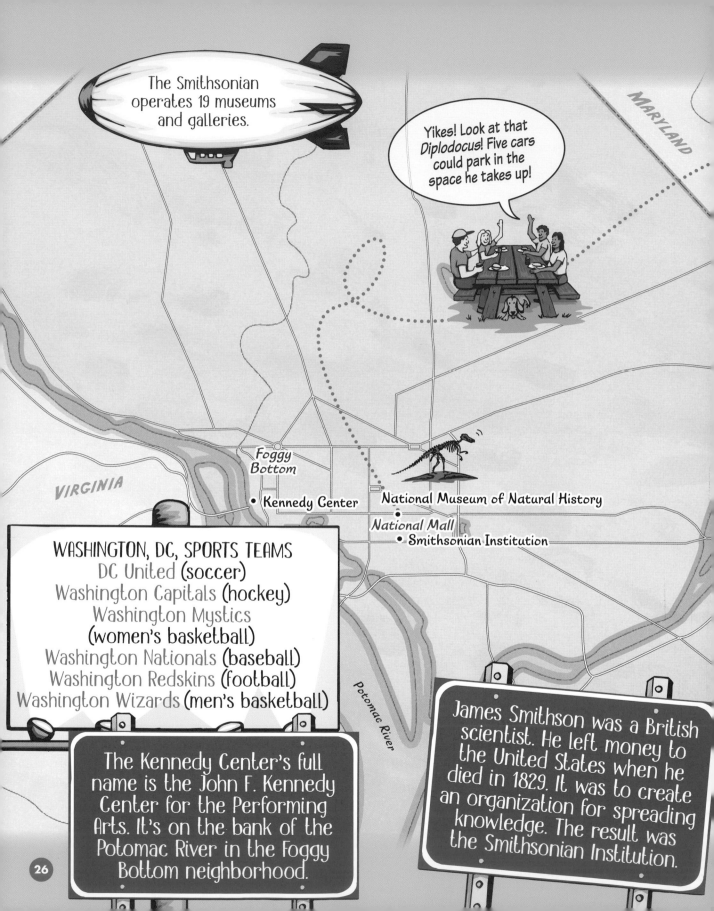

The *Allosaurus* is ready to strike. The *Tyrannosaurus* is ready to bite. Help!

Don't run off just yet. You're safe from attack. You're visiting the National Museum of Natural History! Its dinosaur hall is packed with frightful creatures.

Many museums line the National Mall. One is the National Museum of Natural History. It's part of the Smithsonian Institution.

Visitors love Washington, DC's museums. They enjoy shows at the Kennedy Center, too. Are you a sports fan? There's plenty for you to see. The city has several great teams you can watch.

The National Museum of Natural History is free to visit. It's home to 126 million artifacts!

THE NATIONAL AIR AND SPACE MUSEUM

Do you dream of flying and exploring space? You're not alone. The mysteries of flight have always excited humans. Just visit the National Air and Space Museum. You'll learn how dreams of flight became real!

You'll see the Wright brothers' 1903 plane. They invented the first power-driven aircraft. You'll see the nose of the *Spirit of Saint Louis*. This plane was flown across the Atlantic Ocean in 1927. And you'll gaze at *Apollo 11*. It took the first U.S. astronauts to the moon!

If you visit, get there early. More than 8,000,000 people visit every year!

The Spirit of Saint Louis *was last flown on April 30, 1928.*

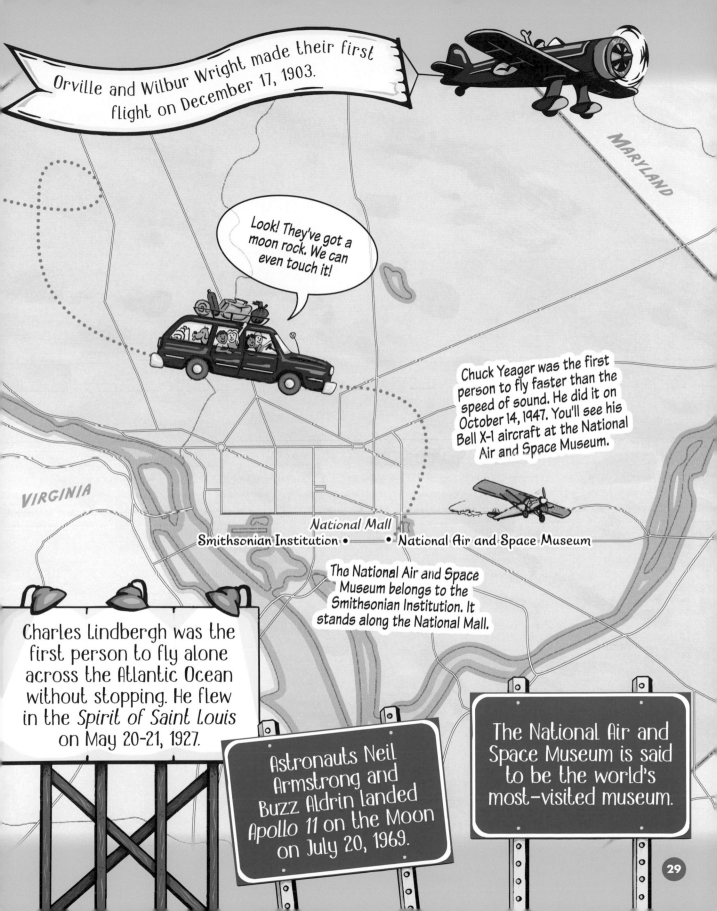

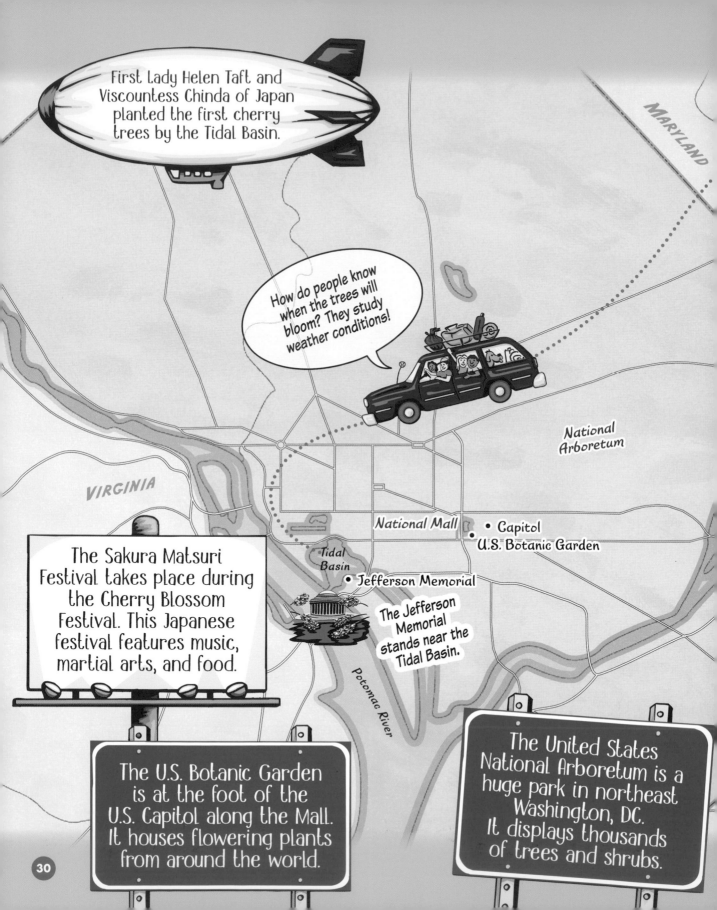

CHERRY BLOSSOM TIME

Is it springtime? Then it's cherry blossom time!

Approximately 3,750 cherry trees grow near the Potomac. The best-known trees surround the Tidal Basin. That's a pond just south of the National Mall. The first trees were planted in 1912. They were gifts from the people of Japan.

The pink and white flowers are awesome. When's the best time to see them? During the Cherry Blossom Festival! It's held in late March and early April. It attracts thousands of people from around the world.

Spring is in the air! Cherry trees blossom near the Jefferson Memorial.

The printing presses buzz and whir. Big sheets of paper zoom through them. Then the paper is cut. What's the finished product? Money!

You're touring the Bureau of Engraving and Printing. It's just east of the Tidal Basin. It prints our paper money. You'll see millions of dollars there!

Washington, DC, doesn't have many factories. The main factory activities are printing and publishing. Most printing is done for the government. Printing money is one example. Many government documents need to be printed, too. The U.S. Government Publishing Office does this job.

Need some extra cash? Dollar bills are printed at the Bureau of Engraving and Printing.

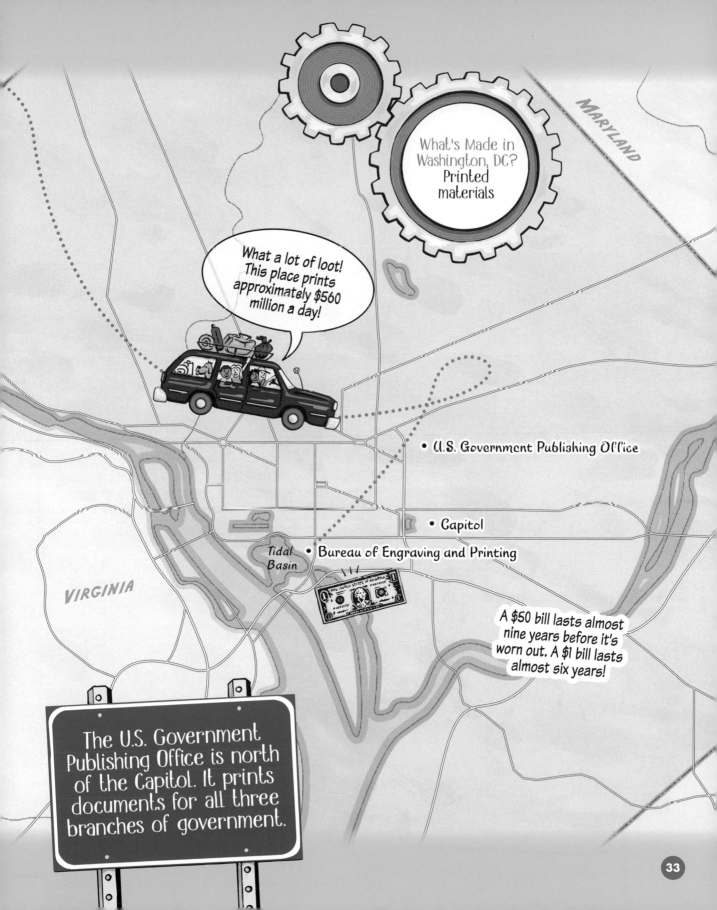

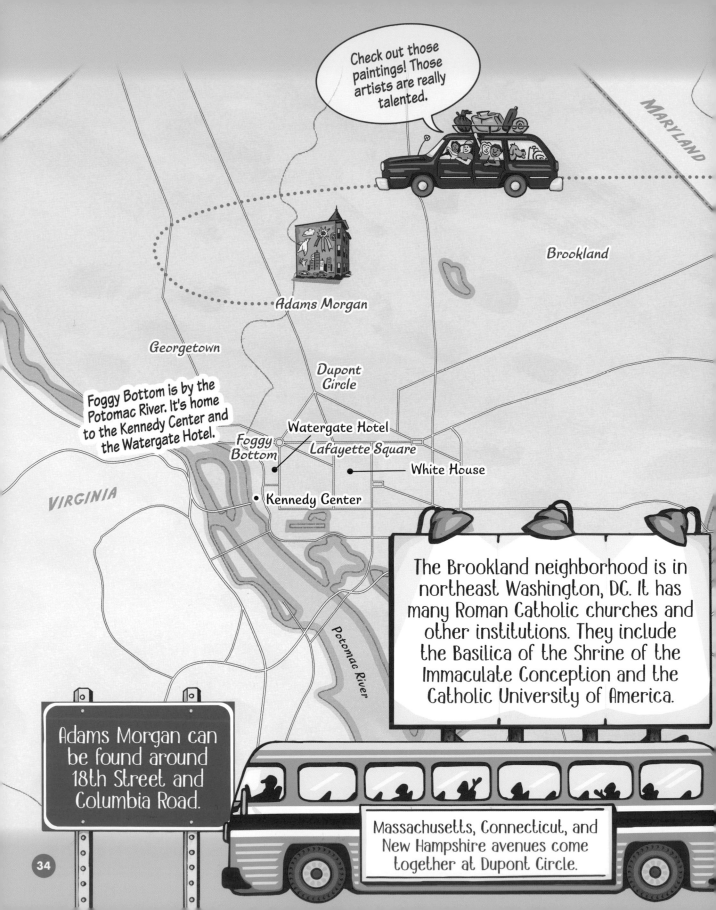

Check out those paintings! Those artists are really talented.

MARYLAND

Brookland

Adams Morgan

Georgetown

Dupont Circle

Foggy Bottom is by the Potomac River. It's home to the Kennedy Center and the Watergate Hotel.

Watergate Hotel

Lafayette Square

Foggy Bottom

White House

VIRGINIA

Kennedy Center

Potomac River

The Brookland neighborhood is in northeast Washington, DC. It has many Roman Catholic churches and other institutions. They include the Basilica of the Shrine of the Immaculate Conception and the Catholic University of America.

Adams Morgan can be found around 18th Street and Columbia Road.

Massachusetts, Connecticut, and New Hampshire avenues come together at Dupont Circle.

Cruise through Adams Morgan. That's a neighborhood in northwest Washington, DC. The area is home to many **Hispanic** people. You'll see huge, colorful murals, or wall paintings.

Some paintings show people working or playing. Others show animals or historic figures. Washington, DC, has many other interesting neighborhoods. Many are named for the circles and squares they are by. Wealthy people first built up the area around Dupont Circle. Now the area has many **embassies** and museums.

The Lafayette Square neighborhood is near the White House. Georgetown is known for its shops and restaurants. The city has many more neighborhoods.

Some murals include past presidents.

OUR TRIP

We visited many amazing places on our trip! We also met a lot of interesting people along the way. Look at the map below. Use your finger to trace all the places we have been.

How many animals live in the National Zoo? *See page 9 for the answer.*

Who was Georgetown possibly named after? *Page 10 has the answer.*

When was New York City the nation's capital? *See page 13 for the answer.*

What kinds of statues does Statuary Hall feature? *Look on page 15 for the answer.*

How many rooms are in the White House? *Page 17 has the answer.*

Where was Abraham Lincoln shot? *Turn to page 21 for the answer.*

What did Chuck Yeager do in 1947? *Look on page 29 for the answer.*

How long does a $50 bill last before it wears out? *Turn to page 33 for the answer.*

MARYLAND

Rock Creek Park

Adams Morgan

WASHINGTON, DC

Georgetown

Lincoln Memorial

White House

National Archives

National Museum of Natural History

National Mall

Capitol

Washington Monument

National Air and Space Museum

Bureau of Engraving and Printing

Tidal Basin

VIRGINIA

Potomac River

Anacostia Community Museum

OFFICIAL SYMBOLS

Bird: Wood thrush

Flower: American beauty rose

Tree: Scarlet oak

Official seal

OFFICIAL SONG

"WASHINGTON"

Words and music by Jimmie Dodd

Washington, the fairest city in the greatest land of all,
Named for one, our country's father who first answered freedom's call,
God bless our White House, our Capitol too,
and keep ever flying the Red, White and Blue,

Grandest spot beneath the sun is Washington.

Oh the cherry blossoms bring a lot of joy each Spring,
and the statue of Abe Lincoln greets your eye,

When parades pass in review down Pennsylvania Avenue,
ev'rybody lifts their voices to the sky!

Washington, the fairest city in the greatest land of all,
Named for one, our country's father who first answered freedom's call,
God bless our White House, our Capitol too,
and keep ever flying the Red, White and Blue,
Grandest spot beneath the sun is Washington.

That was a great trip! We have traveled all over Washington, DC! There are a few places that we didn't have time for, though. Next time, we plan to visit the International Spy Museum! Visitors can learn all about the history of spies around the world. The museum even has real spy artifacts on display!

Official flag

FAMOUS PEOPLE

Albee, Edward (1928–2016), playwright

Bernstein, Carl (1944–), journalist

C. K., Louis (1967–), comedian and actor

Chappelle, Dave (1973–), comedian and actor

Chung, Connie (1946–), television newscaster

Danziger, Paula (1944–2004), children's author

Davis, Benjamin Oliver, Jr. (1912–2002), leader of the Tuskegee Airmen

Davis, Benjamin Oliver, Sr. (1877–1970), first African American general

Dulles, John Foster (1888–1959), lawyer and diplomat

Durant, Kevin (1988–), professional basketball player

Ellington, Duke (1899–1974), jazz musician

Gaye, Marvin (1939–1984), singer and songwriter

Gore, Al (1948–), former U.S. vice president

Hawn, Goldie (1945–), actor

Hoover, J. Edgar (1895–1972), first director of the FBI

Jackson, Samuel L. (1948–), actor

Kennedy, John Fitzgerald, Jr. (1960–1999), lawyer and publisher

Leonard, Sugar Ray (1956–), boxer

Luck, Andrew (1989–), professional football player

Nye, Bill (1955–), American science educator and television presenter

Sousa, John Philip (1854–1932), composer

Williams, Anthony (1951–), politician

WORDS TO KNOW

amendments (uh-MEND-muhnts) changes or additions

civil rights (SIV-il RITES) the rights of a citizen

colonists (KOL-uh-nists) people who settle a new land for their home country

diagonal (dye-AG-uh-nuhl) a slanted line

embassies (EM-buh-seez) offices of representatives of foreign countries

engineer (en-juh-NIHR) someone who designs or builds machines, vehicles, bridges, roads, or other structures

Hispanic (hiss-PAN-ik) coming from or having to do with countries where Spanish is spoken

industry (IN-duh-stree) a type of business

inland (IN-luhnd) away from coastal areas

minister (MIN-uh-stur) a representative of a foreign country

monument (MON-yuh-muhnt) a large marker that honors a person or event

quadrants (KWAH-druhnts) sections created by cutting a circle into four equal parts

suburbs (SUHB-urbz) communities at the edge or just outside of a large city

TO LEARN MORE

IN THE LIBRARY

Korrell, Emily B. *Awesome Adventures at the Smithsonian: The Official Kids Guide to the Smithsonian Institution*. Washington, DC: Smithsonian Books, 2013.

Ogintz, Eileen. *The Kid's Guide to Washington, DC*. Guilford, CT: Globe Pequot, 2013.

Singer, Allison. *What Is the President's Job?* New York, NY: DK Publishing, 2017.

ON THE WEB

Visit our Web site for links about Washington, DC:

childsworld.com/links

Note to Parents, Teachers, and Librarians: We routinely verify our Web links to make sure they are safe and active sites. So encourage your readers to check them out!

PLACES TO VISIT OR CONTACT

DC Visitor Information Center

washington.org
901 7th Street NW, 4th Floor
Washington, DC 20001
202/789.7000

For more information about visiting Washington, DC

The Historical Society of Washington, DC

dchistory.org
801 K Street NW
Washington, DC 20001
202/249-3955

For more information about the history of Washington, DC

Washington, DC, covers 68 square miles (177 sq km). It's smaller in size than any state.

INDEX

Bye, Capital City. We had a great time. We'll be back soon!